Edition limited to 1200 numbered copies
of which 500, together with 100 signed by the author,
are for publication in Great Britain
by Faber and Faber Limited
and 500, together with 100 signed by the author,
are for publication in the United States of America
by E. P. Dutton and Company Inc.
This copy is Number

657

THE RED LIMBO LINGO

LAWRENCE DURRELL

The Red Limbo Lingo

A Poetry Notebook

FABER AND FABER

3 Queen Square

London

First published in 1971
by Faber and Faber Limited
London WC1
Printed in Great Britain at
The Curwen Press Plaistow
All rights reserved

ISBN 0 571 09723 5

ISBN 0 571 09724 3
(Signed Limited Edition)

FOR MIRIAM CENDRARS

First of all,
He did not ask to be born.
He did not ask to find himself in the Red Limbo—
Nine months awash in the seablue sac
Of the amnion, once there and back:
Washed ashore in the bulrushes of an ape's wish.
When he reached civilisation the gallows was
Still warm; some unacknowledged legislator
Must have been at work. Give us this way
Our daily noose.
Nine months of the blood's imprinting finely
In the womb had filled his charts with lines;
Pumped and ladled rich spagyrick blood
Direct into the plexus where all the dark
Foreknowledge will abide and henceforth be . . .

A destiny predetermined by his
Limbotalk and limbothink
He learned how to lovejingle the limbs' lingo,
Even he hit headlines some-once like
A punpampered pimp in a sunburst of
Aeroplane eyewash; simply to try and find a way
Through the whole unscripted and quite
Untabulated cryptic fauna posed against
Its tapestry of carnal violence.
Because he was free he was bound,
By double sex and double axe,
By sun's waning and moon's mighty wax.

Drunk from the shameless garrick of lovelingo.
Poem?

In fields of flowering cortisone
Could never call his soul his own.
As lover he would have to face
The foul repressions of the race,
As journalist must always brag
Of blood, vagina and the flag.
In the open prison of the gut,
The visions of Tiresias shut.

The primal scene, the primal scene
Often heard but seldom seen
Is always taking place offstage
In something like the lion's cage.

Boy goats girl, and girl gets goat,
The royal yoga of the stoat.

In the Red Limbo Lingo hearts are flowers,
Computers pick them through the sleepy hours,
A pleasant harvest, the machines invest
No terror in the average breast.

What was he to do—indignantly finding himself born
into a race which, despising the idol-worshipping savage,
offered him in exchange the extraordinary blood-spattered

figure of a man nailed to a wooden cross, like an expiring frog. He asked himself 'What could we learn about people who could select this kind of bloody squirming thing as an idol?'

What he learned he did not like.
What he learned he did not like.

Who was this white crucified fish?

He recognised him at long last for a poor homeless vampire who had thrown his splasm-hunger across the span of a thousand years and more, as a ventriloquist throws his voice. He was the symbol of the cannibal sacrament which had established the pedigree of the chosen race, the poets. Even today in the great churches they are still drinking by blood group. It is thicker than water, more exciting to lap than wine. The symbolic flesh is pleasant to munch. This mithraic dream held all history paralysed.

The dreamer on the cross dreams blood.

✲ · ✲ · ✲

The cult of the dead vampire still holds the stage; it begins with the crucifixion, which was the common fate of the vampire in classical times. The symbolism of the event is clear to read, he thought; the crown of thorns, the stake through the side.

Fear, 'that highly dependable emotion', is still there, but its sources change.

In the beginning was the Word, and the word was blood . . .

✲ · ✲ · ✲

Paunches and theology go hand in hand. The belly increases in splendour as the work of art rises in the oven.

✵ · ✵ · ✵

Thought-clusters, constellations of ideas linked by private associations, characterise poetic thinking as against the ratiocinative, noetical operations of philosophers. In this dossier his speculations (which were devoted to wondering what our culture is all about) concerned the symbolic meaning of blood.

The crucifixion as prelude to a love-feast.

✵ · ✵ · ✵

Ideograms, then, of heraldic sense in the alchemical mode; not algebras, children of substitution, changelings of empty motive.

✵ · ✵ · ✵

The poet, that faithful and abundant man, knows to what degree things can unhappen; the perfecting of communications has unexpectedly increased human loneliness. Wishing is leprosy. A poet may start at the end of his diary and work back towards the present.

✵ · ✵ · ✵

Some pretty whipstress in a cotton shift will bare her butt for Sasha's whipcaress. The priceless distinction of solitude is his alone. How would you set about thanking life?

sumptuous lions
brief toads
telephoning giraffes

apt as various fleshes
recent as horses
lucrative as swans

Even the infant's kisses are little rehearsals for dying; how should he cure an impulse to live in castles? The mind-cradles of sleep are beckoning. The protection of sleep by dreaming. Poetry is death's arbitration and living's siphon.

A fat commonplace, a senior *colon*, irascible as only lobsters dare. (The French will tread what angels fear to.) At last, spattered by epigrams he retired to his dungeon and sat in a brood, stomach resting on his knees. Another time he invented a cuddle-mixture for early swans; wrote poetry on his computer or triteness-machine. The poet unlike the computer answers an unasked question in his work. Imprints the soft flesh of language with his love bites. He knows that women are as important as ice cream in hot weather—not essential but very nice if eaten with a spoon. My friend, what are you saying?

The mountain of bloody rags below the guillotine was rapidly distributed; served as talismans, in fertility rites, as ex votos, and perhaps for blacker magics. In the east the marriage sheets with their bloodstains are hung outside the house with cries of acclaim and joy. Astarte was a naked girl riding a white foal with the menstrual blood trickling down her thighs. She rode down to the sea, urging her horse into the curling salt wave.

✲ · ✲ · ✲

The Sacrament as a redemption!

Redemption? From what? We know only too well. The blood of Easter lambs smearing the doorposts of the faithful in Greek islands. Also another echo. The scarlet inks in which only Emperors and Patriarchs and Ambassadors Plenipotentiary may sign protocols. A secret compact with the powers of this world. (Spoken words are hidden from persons not intended to hear them—so says the alchemist.) The Imperial purple-dark venous blood.

✲ · ✲ · ✲

A contraction of the oath 'By Our Lady' gives us the swear word 'Bloody'

Incubus and Succubus
Forever hover over us.

The vampire's distress signal a thick bubbling sound ending on a sob. But when the wound is drawing nicely a low humming *mm mm mm mm*

✲ · ✲ · ✲

Vamps like dry rock-tombs in which to drowse away the daytime hours. They fear the damp. The entrance may be stopped with a light piece of stone, preferably pumice. (Apparently disparate lines of enquiry converging upon a target question.) Other vampire lore. The only oath which binds them is 'Upon my winding sheet'. The trickling blood from the nailholes keeps humanity permanently alerted to the needs of the blood. But they become distressed by the noise of guns fired over water (modern Greek note).

The ubiquitous blood-sacrament stretches up as far as the Faustian compact—to return after death like the Apostles and drink the blood of the living. Guilt and redemption are the natural by-products of this; stronger blood was called for—distilled from the grape—so that humanity might still its disquiets. The alcoholism of poets may be explained thus—they have seen the full horror of the human predicament. From the Virgin Mary to Jeanne d'Arc the continuous line of this preoccupation runs. It has got itself mixed up with the alphabet, with the 28 day menstrual cycle, with the calendar.

O God! We would turn aside from all this and go and live with three little houris called Orifice, Hypotenuse and Eclampsia.

The day which we call today will tomorrow become yesterday; tomorrow will become today in twenty-four hours. Is Time then a superfluous concept?

PO—E—SIE
Manque de Peau
Pot de fleurs
A fleur de peau
Manque de pot
Pot de chambre
Pot de rouge
Coup de Vampire
Qui Sont Donc Les Vampires?
Tête de cire
Peur bleue
Transpiration verte
Mais ils pissent rouge.

Of course, he discovered, analysis makes one thirsty; the sacramental blood-spilling of the creative act brings on dizzy spells. The associative calculus runs clear away to blood-guilt in every age; even its taste echoed sperm and sea salt like a younger son. Why then, analogical thinking not analytical thinking! Symbols remembered in perfusion; an index of ideograms subsumed in some perfumed garden where the dirtiest bush could connive a flower.

> The birds sing lovelingoes in the night
> And the remissive punished lovers
> Each in his graphic state
> Lie awake to ancient radio songs,
> The life-screwing cracknel of a jazz.
> No. He would set up his own idols,
> Grey wave-washed stone of Greece and
> Perhaps one quiet factionless star.

Man is the only species which has done away with sacrificial periodicity in his sexual life, and with it a natural order and an identity with nature.

Every drop of sperm should weigh a ton and does so when it is thought and love-directed.

✳ · ✳ · ✳

Les sangsuelles, on les paie trop chair. Abri des indiscrets. Mon Dieu, quel travail de sape.

He knew now he was of some hectic persuasion, felt the icy priapism which had set in over the earth; cold chimes of the spermatic duct when woman's genitals become hyper-aemic through too ample secretions.

It is not generally known that words, if cut open, will also bleed; a poem of pith may at once accuse, persuade and assuage. The Red Limbo Lingo holds a bloody flag up to nature.

Tamped bull's blood mixed with earth formed the floor of the temple; in Africa still the house of the king is floored in this way. Why, even the concrete around Buckingham Palace is red, to show that it is a royal house. In Provence you bury an animal under a cherry tree to nourish the fruit with mammal's blood. Or the blood-count with its red and white chromosomes, war of the Roses, Tudor and Plantagenet, leukaemia, metastasis.

✳ · ✳ · ✳

The invitation to 'come down to the abattoir for a warm glass' was no joke in fin-de-siècle Paris as the prints attest. If you were looking a little pale after a night of folly, or were disposed to tuberculosis, it was customary to go down

17

B

to La Villette. A cow was hobbled and an incision was made in its side; a glass captured the hissing blood. The women laughed and charmingly accepted their glasses. They toasted love!

The Roman patrician refreshed himself with the blood of the losing gladiator.

Before the first World War cases of epilepsy were sometimes treated at the scaffold during a capital execution.

Transfusion! Now it has been brought to perfection and is applied on a very large scale; it enjoys very much success, as much on the part of the donors as on that of the receivers.

The Masai value blood as a staple, which renders them as ferocious and warlike as Christians. Drink up. Time, gentlemen, please.

> *Les Vampires dînent très tard*
> *Et ils jouissent seuls.*
> *Ils nous enseignent de saigner,*
> *Signez, poète, saigner saigner signer . . .*
> *Il faut s'obstiner de s'abstenir*
> *Il faut s'abstenir de s'obstiner.*

We speak in puns and ellipses lest the computers, our children, overhear; but is there any blood left in the cut word?

> Epitaph for the Tomb of
> a Red Limbo Lingo poet-vampire

'Pas sérieux s'abstenir'.

Taking stock he found all he had with which to face this state of things was:

Heartbeats	70 a minute
Breaths	900 an hour or 15 a minute
Breaths	21,600 a day
Life span:	60 years

✡ · ✡ · ✡

He asked himself who first thought of punctuating time. The memory of unpunctuated process still hangs on in the unconscious—the first timepieces were shaped like an egg.

✡ · ✡ · ✡

He also noted gravely about how history grew absurd by becoming too serious. A grocer carried away by a cannonball. A diplomat bitten by a frog in a lift.

La mort avance
La vie recule
Ce soir j'épouse
La noctambule.

Taillez votre prunier
Mais taillez en bol
Quand la sève monte, chérie
Baby must fall,
Top it and tail it
And pop it in a pot.
When the bough breaks, chérie
Baby must rot.

Small babies on their beds of nails
Are practising a character
By longitude and latitude
In silence or in lassitude
Circumference to diameter
The spirit levels of the mind
Professional and amateur
Are practising a character.

He bowed down to:

Give us this day our
Annual increment
Hourly excrement
Daily sacrament.

An igneous old moon crawls out.
Flies trapped in a wine decanter boom,
Diagram of jazz in a furnished room.
All night he sits at open chessboards
Flying through all his huge inner space
Clad in the same old tunic of blood and muscle,
The tribe's bruised heartbeat hovering
Always around love yet always
Foundering in capital disgrace.

He was interested only in the sublime, whether
it were good or evil.

longue langue
chère chair
touche tache
every where
he was here
she was there
cible sensible
amour amer

She whooped him up with the Song of Songs
then put him out like a stub.

So he woke at last the slumbering only
Rose: black as the very blood of prose,
Sweet as a negro ember burning,
Red as the taste of learning,
Bitter as we suppose.
Replacing one scourge with another,
For the red rose was the vampire's mother.
By any other name is known—
Adonais' blood, it was his own.

The calendars of barbers carefully set out the
times propitious to bleeding, when the Moon
was in Aries, Libra, Sagittarius or Pisces.
Cupid gave Harpocrates (God of Silence) a
rose as a bribe to conceal the amours of Venus.
It became the symbol of silence, was sculptured
on the ceilings of banqueting halls to remind
guests that what was spoken *sub vino* was not
to be uttered aloud.
>Sub rosa
>Subrosicrucifixion
>The alchemist's ur-fiction.

THE RECKONING

Later some of these heroic worshippers
May live out one thrift in a world of options,
The crown of thorns, the bridal wreath of love,
Desires in all their motions.
'As below, darling, so above.'
In one thought focus and resume
The thousand contradictions,
And still with a sigh these warring fictions.

Timeless as water into language flowing,
Molten as snow on new burns,
The limbo of half-knowing
Where the gagged conscience twists and turns,
Will plant the flag of their unknowing.

It is not peace we seek but meaning.

To convince at last that all is possible,
That the feeble human finite must belong
Within the starry circumference of wonder,
And waking alone at night so suddenly
Realise how careful one must be with hate—
For you become what you hate too much,
As when you love too much you fraction
By insolence the fine delight . . .

It is not meaning that we need but sight.

NOBODY

You and who else?
Who else? Why Nobody.
I shall be weeks or months away now
Where the diving roads divide,
A solitude with little dignity,
Where forests lie, where rivers pine,
In a great hemisphere of loveless sky:
And your letters will cross mine.

Somewhere perhaps in a cobweb of skyscrapers
Between fifth and sixth musing I'll go,
Matching some footprints in young snow,
Within the loving ambush of some heart,
So close and yet so very far apart . . .
I don't know, I just don't know.

Two beings watching the spyscrapers fade,
Rose in the falling sleet or
Phantom green, licking themselves
Like great cats at their toilet,
Licking their paws clean.
I shall hesitate and falter, that much I know.

Moreover, do you suppose, you too
When you reach India at last, as you will,
I'll be back before two empty coffee cups
And your empty chair in our shabby bistro;
You'll have nothing to tell me either, no,
Not the tenth part of a sigh to exchange.
Everything will be just so.
I'll be back alone again
Confined in memory, but nothing to report,
Watching the traffic pass and
Dreaming of footprints in the New York snow.

RAIN, RAIN, GO TO SPAIN

That noise will be the rain again,
Hush-falling absolver of together—
Companionable enough, though, here abroad:
The log fire, some conclusive music, loneliness.
I can visualise somebody at the door
But make no name or shape for such an image,
Just a locus for small thefts
As might love us both awake tomorrow,
An echo off the lead and ownerless.
But this hissing rain won't improve anything.
The roads will be washed out. Thinking falters.

My book-lined walls so scholarly,
So rosy, glassed in by the rain.
I finger the sex of many an uncut book.
Now spring is coming you will get home
Later and later in another climate.
You vanished so abruptly it took me by surprise.
I heard to relearn everything again
As if blinded by a life of tiny braille.

Then a whole year with just one card,
From Madrid. 'It is raining here and
Greco is so sombre. I have decided
At last to love nobody but myself.'
I repeat it in an amused way
Sometimes very late at night.
In an amazed way as anyone might
Looking up from a classic into all the
Marvellous rain-polished darkness.

As if suddenly you had gone
Beyond the twelfth desire:
You and memory both become
Contemporary to all this inner music.
Time to sift out our silences, then:
Time to relay the failing fire.

APHROS MEANING SPUME

Aphros Aphrodite the sperm-born one
Could not collect her longings, she had only one,
Soft as a lettuce to the sound,
A captive of one light and longing
Driven underground.

Sadness is only a human body
Seeking the arbitration of heaven,
In the wrong places, under the rose,
In the unleavened leaven.

Tell what wistful kisses travel
Over the skin-heaven of the mind
To where an *amor fati* waits
With fangs drawn back, to bleed
Whoever she can find.

But vines lay no eggs, honey,
And even apostles come to their senses
Sooner or later you may find.
The three Themes of this witchcraft
Are roses, faeces and vampires.
May they bring you a level mind.

A WINTER OF VAMPIRES

From a winter of vampires he selects one,
Takes her to a dark house, undresses her:
It is not at all how the story-books say
But another kind of reversed success.
A transaction where the words themselves
Begin to bleed first and everything else follows.

The dissolution of the egg
In the mind of the lady suggests new
Paths to follow, less improbable victories,
Just as illusory as the old, I fear.
Well, but when the embraces go astray,
When you finger the quick recipes
Of every known suggestion, why,
The whole prosperity of the flesh may be in question.

PISTOL WEATHER

About loving, and such kindred matters
You could be beguiling enough;
Delicacy, constancy and depth—
We examined every artificial prison,
And all with the necessary sincerity, yes.

Some languages have little euphemisms
Which modify suddenly one's notions,
Alter one's whole way of adoring:
Such as your character for 'death',
Which reads simply 'A stepping forever
Into a whiteness without remission.'
With no separation-anxiety I presume?

Surely to love is to coincide a little?
And after I contracted your own mightier
Loneliness, I became really ill myself.
But grateful for the thorny knowledge of you;
And thank you for the choice of time and place.

I would perhaps have asked you away
To my house by the sea, to revive us both,
In absolute solitude and dispassionately,
But all the time I kept seeing the severed head,
Lying there, eyes open, in your lap.

LAKE MUSIC

Deep waters hereabouts.
We could quit caring.
Deep waters darling
We could stop feeling,
You could stop sharing
But neither knife nor gun
From the pockets of mischance pointing;
How slowly we all sink down
This lustful anointing
Ankles first and thighs.
The beautiful grenades
Breasts up to lips and eyes
The vertebrae of believing
And the deep water moving
We could abandon supposing
We could quit knowing
Where we have come from
Where we are going.

STOIC

I, a slave, chained to an oar of poem,
Inhabiting this faraway province where
Nothing happens. I wouldn't want it to.
I have expressly deprived myself of much:
Conversation, sweets of friendship, love . . .
The public women of the town don't appeal.
I wouldn't want them to. There are no others,
At least for an old, smelly, covetous bookman.
So many things might have fed this avocation,
But what's the point? It's too late.

About the matter of death I am convinced,
Also that peace is unattainable and destiny
Impermeable to reason. I am lucky to have
No grave illness, I suppose, no wounds
To ache all winter. I do not drink or smoke.
From all these factors I select one, the silence
Which is that jewel of divine futility,
Refusal to bow, the unvarnished grain
Of the mind's impudence: you see it so well
On the faces of self-reliant dead.

?

Waters rebribing a new moon are all
Dissenting mirrors ending in themselves.

Go away, leave me alone.

Someone still everywhere nearby
So full of fervent need the mouth
The jewelry of smiling: a confession,
Tidemarks of old intentions' dying fall,
Surely that is all now, that is all?

People don't want the experience
Any more: they want an explanation,
How you go about it, when and why.

But all you can say is: Look, it's manifest
And nobody's to blame: it has no name.

Spades touch a buried city,
Calm bodies suffocated by ashes
It happened so quickly there was no time,
Their minds were overrun
The sentry stiffened over a jammed gun,
And waters bribing a new moon are all
The flesh's memories beyond recall.

The voice may have come from a cloud
But more likely the garden's wet planes
A bird or a woman calling in the mist
Asking if anything remains, and if so

c

Which witch? Which witch? Witch!
I am the only one who knows.

SIXTIES

The year his heart wore out—
It was not you nor you
Distributing the weight
Of benefits of doubt.
A surgeon season came
And singled loving out.
A power-cut in a vein
To abruptly caption stone,
And echoing in the mind
Some mindless telephone.

Prophets of discontent,
Impenetrable shades
It was not you nor you
Nor something left unsaid
To elaborate the night,
But a corn-sifting wind
Was never far behind.
Be steadfast where you are
Now, in the sibyllic mind,
His one companionable star.

It was not you nor you
The year his heart wore out
But cryptic as a breath
One crystal changed its hue;
Thus words in music drown,
Comparisons are few,
Nor will we ever know,
Tellurian loveliness,
Which way the fearless waters flow
That softly fathom you.

AVIS

How elapsing our women
Bought with lullaby money
To fill with moon-fluids,
To goad quench and drench with
Quicksilver of druids
Each nonpareil wench.

How spicy their blood is
How tiny their hands
They were netted like quail
In faraway lands.

Come, pretty little ogre
With the fang in your lip
Lest time in its turnings
Should give us the slip.

ONE PLACE

Commission silence for a line or two,
These walls, these trees—time out of mind
Are temples to perfection lightly spent,
Sunbribed and apt in their shadowy stresses,
Where the planes hang heads, lies
Something the mind caresses;
And then—hardly noticed at noon
Bells bowling, the sistrum bonged
From steeples half asleep in bugle water.
(This part to be whispered only.)

To go or stay is really not the question;
Nor even to go forever, one can't allow here
Death as a page its full relapse.
In such a nook it would always be perhaps,
Dying with no strings attached—who could do that?

REVENANTS

Supposing once the dead were to combine
Against us with a disciplined hysteria.
Particular ghosts might then trouble
With professional horrors like
Corpses in evening dress,
Photoglyphs from some ancient calendar
Pictographs of lost time.
The smile frail as a toy night-light
Beside a sleeping infant's bed.
The pallor would be unfeigned,
The child smile in its sleep.

To see them always in memory
Descending a spiral staircase slowly
With that peculiar fond regard

Or else out in silent gardens
Under stone walls, a snapped fountain,
Wild violets there uncaring
Wild cyclamen uncurling
In silence, in loaf-leisure.

Or a last specialised picture
Flickering on the retina perhaps
The suave magnificence of a late
Moon, trying not to insist too much.
Emotions are just pampered mirrors,
Thriftless provinces, penurious settlers.
How to involve all nature in every breath?

THE LAND

The rapt moonwalkers or mere students
Of the world-envelope are piercing
Into the earth's crust to punctuate
Soils and waters with cherished trees
Or cobble with vines, they know it;
Yet have never elaborated a philosophy
Of finite time. I wonder why? Those
Who watch late over the lambs, whom sleep
Deserts because there's thunder in the air.
Just before dawn the whole of nature
Growls in a darkness of impatience.
The season-watchers just march on
Inventing pruning-hooks, winnowing fans
Or odd manual extensions like the spade
Inside the uniform flow of the equinoxes
Not puzzled any more, having forgotten
How brief and how precarious life was,
But finding it chiefly true yet various,
With no uncritical submission to the Gods.

39

JOSS

Perfume of old bones,
Indian bones distilled
In these slender batons;
A whiff of brown saints,
An Indian childhood. Joss.

More mysterious than the opaque
Knuckles of frankincense
The orthodox keep to swamp
Their Easter ikons with today.

The images repeat repent repent (*da capo*)
A second childhood, born again in Greece.
O the benign power, the providing power
Is here too with its reassurance honey.
After the heartbreak of the long voyage,
Same lexicon, stars over the water.

Hello there! Demon of sadness,
You with the coat of many colours,
The necklace of cannibals' teeth.
You with the extravagant arch
To your instep, a woman walking alone
In the reign of her forgiveness
In the rain.

Moi, qui ai toujours guetté le sublime
Me voici de nouveau dans le pétrin,
Hunting the seven keys to human stress,
The search always one minute old,
A single word to transcend all others,
A single name buried excalibur in a stone.

AVIGNON

Come, meet me in some dead café—
A puff of cognac or a sip of smoke
Will grant a more prolific light,
Say there is nothing to revoke.

A veteran with no arm will press
A phantom sorrow in his sleeve;
The aching stump may well insist
On memories it can't relieve.

Late cats, the city's thumbscrews twist.
Night falls in its profuse derision,
Brings candle-power to younger lives,
Cancels in me the primal vision.

Come, random with me in the rain,
In ghastly harness like a dream,
In rainwashed streets of saddened dark
Where nothing moves that does not seem.

INCOGNITO

Outside us smoulder the great
World issues about which nothing
Can be done, at least by us two;
Inside, the smaller area of a life
Entrusted to us, as yet unendowed
Even by a plan for worship. Well,
If thrift should make her worldly
Remind her that time is boundless,
And for call-girls like business-men, money.

Redeem pleasure, then, with a proximate
Love—the other problems, like the ruins
Of man's estate, death of all goodness,
Lie entombed with me here in this
Oldfashioned but convincing death-bed.

Her darkness, her eye are both typical
Of a region long since plunged into
Historic ruin; yet disinherited, she doesn't care
Being perfect both as person and as thing.

All winter now I shall lie suffocating
Under the débris of this thought.

SWIMMERS

Huit heures . . . honte heures . . . supper will be cold.
Sex no substitute for
Science no worship for . . .
At night seeing lights and crouching
Figures round the swimming pool, rapt.
They were fishing for her pearls,
Her necklace had broken while she swam.
'Darling, I bust my pearls.'

But all the time I was away
In sweet and headlong Greece I tried
To write you only the syntax failed,
Each noun became a nascent verb
And all verbs dormant adjectives,
Everything sleeping among the scattered pearls.

Corpses with the marvellous
Property of withoutness
Reign in the whole abundance of the breath.
Each mood has its breathing, so does death.
Soft they sleep and corpsely wise
Scattered the pearls that were their eyes.
Newly mated man and wine
In each others' deaths combine.
Somebody meets everything
While poems in their cages sing.

BLUE

Your ship will be leaving Penang
For Lisbon on the fourteenth,
When I have started pointedly
Living with somebody else.
Yet I can successfully imagine a
Star-crossed circumference of water
Providing a destiny for travellers—
Thoughts neither to pilfer nor squander
During the postcard-troubled nights.

How stable the feeling of being lost grows!
The ocean of memory is ample too,
It wheels about as you crawl over the surface
Of the globe, having cabled away a stormy wish.
Our judgement, our control were beyond all praise.
So prescient were we, it must prove something.

Madam, I presume upon somewhere to continue
Existing round you, say the Indian Ocean
Where life might be fuller of
Such rich machinery that you mightn't flinch;
And how marvellous to be followed
Round the world by a feeling of utter
Sufficiency, tinged a little, I don't doubt,
With self-righteousness, a calming emotion!

I too have been much diminished by wanting;
Now limit my vision to a sufficient loveliness,
To abdicate? But it was never our case,
Though somewhere I feel creep in
The word you said you hated most: 'Nevertheless'.
Well, say it under whatever hostile stars you roam,
Embrace the blue vertigo of the old wish.
And if it gets too much for me
I can always do the other thing, remember?

MISTRAL

At four the dawn mistral usually
A sleep-walking giant sways and crackles
The house, a vessel big with sail.
One head full of poems, cruiser of light,
Cracks open the pomegranate to reveal
The lining of all today's perhapses.

Far away in her carnal fealty sleeps
La Môme in her tiny *chambre de bonne*.
'*Le vent se lève . . . Il faut tenter de vivre.*'

I have grave thoughts about nothingness,
Hold no copyright in Jesus like that girl.
An autopsy would fuse the wires of pleading.
It is simply not possible to thank life.
The universe seems a huge hug without arms.
In foul rapture dawn breaks on grey olives.
Poetry among other afflictions
Is the purest selfishness.

I am making her a small scarlet jazz
For the cellar where they dance
To a wheezy accordion, with a one-eyed man.
Written to a cheeky begging voice.

Moi je suis
Annie Verneuil
Dit Annie La Môme
Parfois je fais la vie
Parfois je chome
Premier Prix de Saloperie
De Paris à Rome
Annie La Môme
Fléau du flic le soir
Sur La Place Vendôme,
Annie Verneuil
Annie La Môme

Freedom is choice: choice bondage.
Where will I next be when the mistral
Rises in sullen trumpets on the hills of bone?

ENVOI

Be silent, old frog.
Let God compound the issue as he must,
And dog eat dog
Unto the final desecration of man's dust.
The just will be devoured by the unjust.